FIFE'S LOST RAILWAYS

Gordon Stansfield

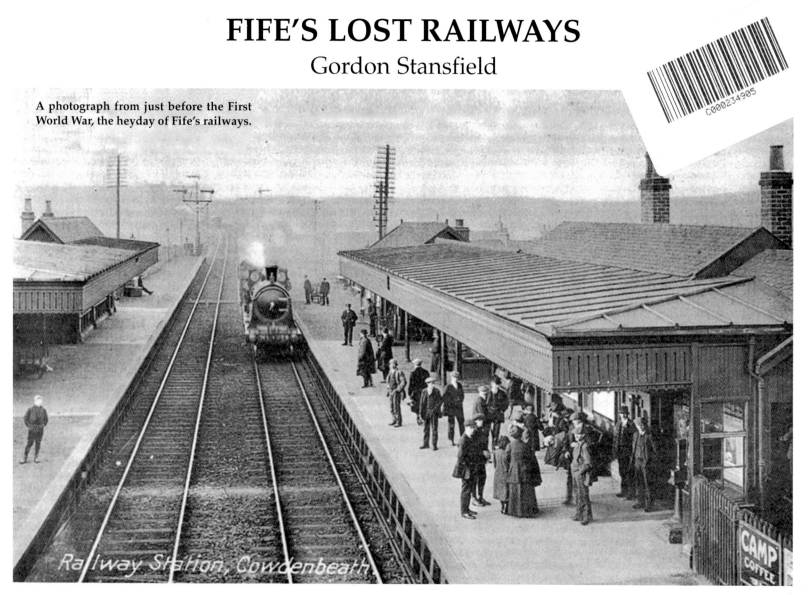

A photograph from just before the First World War, the heyday of Fife's railways.

Railway Station, Cowdenbeath

CAMP COFFEE

Acknowledgements
With the exception of those on pages 5, 6,14,16,17 and 28, all the photographs in this book were taken by W.A.C. Smith and are reproduced here with his kind permission.

The publishers regret that they cannot supply copies of any pictures featured in this book.

A pair of Metro-Cammell sets forming the 10.40 a.m. from Edinburgh to Dundee at Leuchars Junction, August 1958.

INTRODUCTION

The Kingdom of Fife is a very distinct area of Scotland, most of it being sandwiched between two firths and two bridges - the Firth of Tay, traversed by the Tay Bridge, in the north, and the Firth of Forth, crossed by the Forth Bridge, in the south. Agriculture is prominent in the north and east while the southern and western localities are mainly industrial, and a feature of this economic diversity is the spread of larger towns such as Dunfermline and Kirkcaldy in the south, while the north and east mainly contain smaller farming and fishing communities.

When the railways first came to Fife there were no bridges linking the Kingdom with either Dundee or Edinburgh. Back then, Fife was quite a different place and travelling to towns which are easy to reach today was very difficult. For example, the easiest way to reach Edinburgh was actually by passenger ferry. The first proposals to introduce passenger railways to the Kingdom were put forward in 1840, reaching a peak of interest five years later when sixteen schemes were put forward. By this time railway mania was in full swing throughout Scotland and the schemes envisaged in Fife included some which had little hope of ever becoming reality. These included a route known as the Eastern Fife line which was proposed from the then ferry port of Burntisland to Tayport, via Kirkcaldy, Markinch and Cupar, where it would link with the ferry crossing to Dundee. Another proposal, known as the Western Fife Railway, intended to start at Seafield near Kirkcaldy and run inland to Newburgh where it would cross the River Tay before heading west to Perth. Proposals to build a railway line require an Act of Parliament and one such scheme submitted by the Fife and Perth Railway to the House of Commons was thrown out when it was discovered that no proper plans were available.

Finally, in September 1847 the line from Burntisland to Cupar (which today forms part of the east coast line linking Edinburgh with Dundee and Aberdeen) was opened and at last passenger railways became a reality. Other passenger lines and services were established throughout the rest of the nineteenth century and even as late as 1906 a line was built providing a service from Dunfermline to Culross. However, the greatest achievements of this era were the linking of the Kingdom to the rest of the country by the Tay and Forth Bridges. The first Tay Bridge was short-lived, opening in May 1878 and disastrously blown down in December 1879. (The replacement was not completed until 1888.) In 1890 the Forth Bridge was opened and is still regarded as one of the Victorian era's major engineering triumphs.

The dawn of the twentieth century saw Fife's railways at their peak. The North British Railway Company had established itself as the monopoly rail operator by purchasing and taking over small and large railways such as the Edinburgh and Northern and the Edinburgh, Perth and Dundee. (The fact that the North British had built the Forth and Tay Bridges also helped them to dominance.) The network of services opened up new horizons whether you were a coal miner in Leven or a fisherman in Pittenweem. Many lines joined the main rail artery which threaded its way through Fife linking Edinburgh and Dundee and most of these lines remained intact well beyond nationalisation until the 1950s.

The 1960s saw much rationalisation of Fife's rail network. As the motor car became dominant, many parts of the Kingdom lost their rail services for good. However, the railways continue to play a prominent part in local transport as the main trunk route between Edinburgh and Dundee still survives and the Fife circle line provides a service linking Edinburgh, Dunfermline and Glenrothes. It is also still possible to travel across the county to Perth and north to Inverness and new stations have even been opened such as at Dalgety Bay in 1997 and Glenrothes with Thornton in 1992.

Alloa (Kincardine Junction) - Dunfermline (Charlestown Branch Junction)

Passenger service withdrawn	7 July 1930	*Stations closed*	*Date*
Distance	15.5 miles	Kincardine	7 July 1930
		Culross	7 July 1930
Stations closed	*Date*	Torryburn	7 July 1930
Clackmannan and Kennet	7 July 1930	Cairneyhill	7 July 1930
Kilbagie	7 July 1930		

A preserved NBR 4-4-0, no.256 *Glen Douglas*, with an enthusiasts' special at Kincardine Station, June 1960.

The line between Alloa and Dunfermline via Culross was opened in two stages. The first, between Alloa and Kilbagie, was opened on 18 December 1893, while the second stage to Dunfermline was in operation by July 1906. After leaving Alloa in Clackmannanshire, the line entered Fife at Kincardine and then continued eastwards to Dunfermline Lower Station. From this line there was one branch line to Charlestown which closed to passengers in 1926. There was a more direct line from Alloa to Dunfermline via Oakley (Stirling - Dunfermline Lower) which used the station at Dunfermline Upper. (Dunfermline was one of those towns that could boast of having both Upper and Lower stations and these were provided by the railway company for mainly operational reasons; often the geographical position of railway lines entering a town dictated this requirement.) As some of the track on this line remains, the local authority has shown an interest in possibly restarting a passenger service some time in the future.

The Station, Culross, c.1906

Perth (Hilton Junction) - Bridge of Earn (Bridge of Earn Junction) - Cowdenbeath (North Junction)

Passenger service withdrawn	5 January 1970	*Stations closed*	*Date*
Distance	22 miles	Mawcarse	15 June 1964
		Milnathort	15 June 1964
		Kinross Junction	5 January 1970
Stations closed	*Date*	Kinross Junction	June 1890
Bridge of Earn	15 June 1964	Loch Leven	1 September 1921
Bridge of Earn (First)	1 February 1892	Blairadam	22 September 1930
Abernethy Road	25 July 1848	Kelty	22 September 1930
Glenfarg	15 June 1964		

The name Station Road is one of the few reminders that Kelty was once served by a railway.

This line was built in stages with the first, southern, section from Mawcarse to Cowdenbeath opening in June 1860. The southern section was owned by a company called the Fife and Kinross, but they did not have the resources to operate the line in terms of rolling stock so it was operated by another company, the Edinburgh, Perth and Dundee. However, in August 1862 both were taken over by the North British who were rapidly making inroads into Fife. At that time the line was a single track branch line but with the opening of the Forth Bridge the North British had plans to reach Perth. The track was doubled and the remaining section to Bridge of Earn opened in June 1890. The section to Perth had already opened in July 1848 as part of the Perth to Ladybank route. Services usually originated at Inverness or Perth and the line ran through Perthshire, Kinross-shire and Fife before reaching the Forth Bridge. At Kinross Junction Station the Devon Valley line headed westwards towards Dollar and Alloa This line was closed on 15 June 1964.

South of Kinross Junction was Loch Leven which, during the winter months in the early part of this century, was host to curling competitions when the loch was frozen. Special trains were run, often at short notice, for competitors and spectators alike but the popularity of the sport waned after the First World War and Loch Leven Station closed to passengers on 1 September 1921. Blairadam and Kelty Stations at the southern end of the line lost their passenger service in 1930 while those in the northern section, apart from Kinross Junction, lost their service in June 1-964. Mawcarse Station was one such station. At one time it had been a junction and was known as Mawcarse Junction until May 1962 with a line servicing Ladybank but this service was withdrawn in June 1950.

Through trains to Edinburgh continued to use the line up until closure and were then diverted via the Bridge of Earn - Ladybank line which was reopened for this purpose (as it had been closed since September 1955). The only remaining station on the line between 1964 and closure was Kinross Junction (known initially as Kinross until December 1860 and then Hopefield Junction until October 1871). Upon closure the station was quickly demolished in order to make way for the new M90 Motorway. The section of line between Perth (Hilton Junction) and Bridge of Earn was reopened in October 1975 to provide services from Perth to Ladybank (Bridge of Earn - Ladybank).

Bridge of Earn (Bridge of Earn Junction) - Ladybank (Ladybank North Junction)

Passenger service withdrawn	19 September 1955	*Stations closed*	*Date*
Distance	15.25 miles	Newburgh	19 September 1955
		Lindores	9 December 1847
Stations closed	*Date*	Glenbirnie	17 May 1848
Abernethy	19 September 1955	Collesie	19 September 1955

This line was opened on 18 July 1845 by the Scottish Central Railway Company who used it to introduce the first passenger services between Perth and Edinburgh. This was a roundabout route and although it linked the two cities, it was not very direct. Subsequently, the line's importance was reduced to the provision of local services when the North British started their service between Edinburgh and Perth via Kinross Junction in June 1890. From Newburgh there was a branch to St Fort on the Dundee to Edinburgh east coast main line. Trains-using this line often began their journey at Perth and traversed the Bridge of Earn - Ladybank line as far as Newburgh.

When services were withdrawn in 1955, the line was retained for freight traffic. In January 1967 a severe line blockage, caused by a rock fall at Clatchland Craig Quarry, threatened the line's future as the cost of clearing the incident and the availability of alternative routes such as the Perth - Bridge of Earn - Cowdenbeath line could have made British Rail consider permanent closure. However, with the closure of the Perth - Cowdenbeath line, BR decided to retain it. October 1975 saw the re-establishment of passenger services when services between Inverness or Perth and Edinburgh were reintroduced. In the summer of 1998 there were on weekdays six southbound and seven northbound services between Edinburgh, Perth and Inverness (while on Sundays there were two southbound and three northbound).

Ladybank (Ladybank Junction) - Mawcarse Junction

Passenger service withdrawn	5 June 1950	*Stations closed*	*Date*
Distance	11.5 miles	Auchtermuchty	5 June 1950
		Strathmiglo	5 June 1950
		Gateside	5 June 1950

This cross country line linked two main lines these being the one from Edinburgh to Perth via Kinross and the still in use east coast main line from Edinburgh to Dundee. Opened by the Fife and Kinross Railway Company by 1861 the line had 3 intermediate stations. There was in the main a service of 5 trains daily in each direction with some destinations as far afield as Alloa and Stirling. In the decade before passenger services were withdrawn Sentinel Railcars were used for a period. Following closure in the 1960s railtour specials visited the line in 1960 and 1963 hauled by the locomotive *Glen Douglas* built in 1913 by the North British Railway Company and preserved in Glasgow's museum of transport. Freight services continued from Ladybank to Auchtermuchty until 1964.

Charlestown - Dunfermline (Elbowend Junction)

Passenger service withdrawn	1 November 1926	*Stations closed*	*Date*
Distance	4.25 miles	Charlestown	1 November 1926
		Braeside Halt	1 August 1926

After it closed Charlestown Station, near Limekilns, became this house, but the building was derelict by the time of this photograph, September 1968.

Once a Firth of Forth port, the town of Charlestown appears very early in the history of railways in Fife due to the wagon ways that operated between its harbour and nearby coal mines. By the early nineteenth century a line from Dunfermline to Charlestown was certainly operating for passengers wishing to travel by the steamers which were anchored off Charlestown harbour. However, with the advent of the standard railway gauge in the second part of the nineteenth century, the line was rebuilt and came into passenger use on 1 September 1894.

The North British Railway Company had considered using Charlestown as a possible location for the Forth Bridge but decided in the end that Queensferry, was more suitable due to the high approaches which could be made there (the rail line on the bridge is 150 feet above sea level) and greater resources of tough whinstone at the north end of the bridge.

The North British opened a halt at Braeside in September 1921 but there were no freight facilities. After the withdrawal of passenger services in 1926, the line remained open to freight traffic with a service to the Royal Navy Armament Depot at Crombie for many years.

Inverkeithing: North Junction - East Junction

Passenger service withdrawn   24 November 1989   *Distance*   0.25 miles

This short spur formed the north side of a triangle at Inverkeithing which allowed trains to travel from Kirkcaldy (on the east coast main line) to Dunfermline. Although 1989 was the official closure date, passenger services were withdrawn several years earlier and British Rail did not have to go through any statutory closure procedures as there were no stations on this short line.

Freight awaiting departure from the closed station at Leslie, August 1961.

Leslie - Markinch (Markinch Junction)

Passenger service withdrawn   4 January 1932   *Stations closed*   *Date*
Distance   4.25 miles   Leslie   4 January 1932

From 1857 the small town of Leslie was reached by a branch line which left the east coast main line between Edinburgh and Dundee at Markinch. Bus competition in the early 1930s resulted in the passenger service being withdrawn although specials did travel on the line from time to time. Goods traffic continued on the line until October 1967.

Leven - St Andrews

Passenger service withdrawn	6 September 1965	*Stations closed*	*Date*
Distance	28.75 miles	Pittenweem	6 September 1965
		Anstruther (First)	1 September 1883
Stations closed	*Date*	Anstruther	6 September 1965
Leven (First)	1 June 1867	Crail	6 September 1965
Lundin Links	6 September 1965	Kingsbarns	22 September 1930
Largo	6 September 1965	Boarhills	22 September 1930
Kilconquhar	6 September 1965	Stravithie	22 September 1930
Elie	6 September 1965	Mount Melville	22 September 1930
St Monans	6 September 1965	St Andrews (First)	18 August 1857

Class B1, 4-6-0, no. 61342, at Largo with the 11.10 a.m.
from Glasgow (Queen Street) to Crail, July 1964.

This line formed part of the route known as the East Coast of Fife line which ran from St Andrews to Thornton Junction Station. The line passed through many of the fishing villages in the East Neuk and opened in the following stages: Leven to Kilconquhar, July 1857; Kilconquhar to Anstruther, September 1863; Anstruther to Boarhills, September 1883; Boarhills to St Andrews, June 1887. Unlike many lines some of the freight services were withdrawn before the passenger service because freight traffic was so low. The freight service from Boarhills to St Andrews was withdrawn in October 1964 and the remaining ones in July 1966. At one time the line boasted a named express train. Known as the 'Fife Coast Express' it ran from St Andrews to Glasgow in the morning, making the return journey in late afternoon (each journey took just over two hours and forty minutes). The line also had its share of station closures during the First World War with Pittenweem/ Boarhills and Mount Melville being closed from January 1917 until February 1919 due to the lack of manpower available to run stations that had low levels of passenger traffic.

Class B1, 4-6-0, no. 61118, at Kilconquhar with the 2.10 p.m. from Dundee (Tay Bridge) to Edinburgh, April 1957.

A housing estate now stands on the site of Elie Station.

Class J37, 0-6-0, no. 64618, at Elie with the 9.37 a.m. from Glasgow (Queen Street) to Anstruther, July 1959.

St Monans.

A Metro-Cammell triple set forming the 2.42 p.m. from Dundee (Tay Bridge) to Edinburgh at Anstruther, August 1960.

The site of Ansturther Station is now taken
by a small industrial estate and a car park.

There is little trace of the station left today, although the flags of Caithness stone used on the platform now form the path through the town's Scottish Fisheries Museum.

Class B1, 4-6-0, no. 61330, at Crail with the 2.35 p.m. to Thornton Junction, March 1965.

A diesel multiple unit forming the 2.42 p.m. from Dundee to Edinburgh, passing the closed station at Kingsbarns, March 1965.

The station house at Boarhills has
now been replaced by a dwelling.

Class J37, 0-6-0, no. 64602, passing the closed station at Boarhills with an enthusiasts special from Dundee, May 1965.

The closed station at Stravithie, looking east, March 1965.

Class B1, 4-6-0, no. 61133, passing the closed station at Mount Melville with the 2.10 p.m. from Dundee to Edinburgh, August 1958.

Passenger service withdrawn	31 March 1919	*Stations closed*		*Date*
Distance	2 miles	Cowdenbeath Old		31 March 1919

The closed station of Cowdenbeath Old, looking north, February 1960.

This line was closed when a new alignment through Cowdenbeath New Station was opened on 29 March 1919 (and which still serves Lochgelly and Cowdenbeath today). The station at Cowdenbeath Old was known as Cowdenbeath until 1 June 1890 when the New Station opened.

Lochgelly (Lumphinnans Junction) - Kelty (Kelty South Junction)

Passenger service withdrawn   2 June 1890   *Distance*   2 miles

Like the section from Lochgelly to Crossgates, the line from Kelty to Lochgelly was closed to passenger traffic on 2 June 1890 when the new line deviation serving Cowdenbeath New Station was opened.

Class J36, 0-6-0, no.65345, shunting the Lochty Branch freight trip at Montrave, March 1961.

Lochty - Cameron Bridge (Lochty Branch Junction)

Although this branch line never had a regular public passenger service, it was noted as being the longest goods-only railway line in the country. Built by the North British in 1898 and crossing the central part of the Kingdom, the line was known as the East Fife Central Railway and its main traffic was coal and agricultural produce. The North British felt that there was insufficient demand to support a passenger service as the places served had a very low population. However, goods stations were built at Lochty, Largoward, Montrave and Kennoway Siding and these remained in operation until the line closed in August 1964. After closure the line gained a passenger service when a local farmer, John Cameron, purchased from British Rail one and a quarter miles of the line leading up to Lochty. In June 1967 he formed the Lochty Private Railway and the following year passenger services began, using the A4 class locomotive *Union of South Africa*. Rolling stock consisted of an observation car built in 1937 for the Coronation Express on which the *Union of South Africa* had operated. (The Coronation Express were named trains which ran between London King's Cross and Edinburgh Waverley from 1937 onwards. In the summer months these trains had an observation coach added which contained, amongst other attractions, rotating armchairs). A small platform was built at Knightsward on the southern end of the line and since the *Union of South Africa* was retired from service in 1972 a variety of locomotives succeeded it until the line was closed and lifted a few years ago.

Methil - Thornton Junction (Thornton South Junction)

Passenger service withdrawn	10 January 1955	*Stations closed*	*Date*
Distance	5.25 miles	Buckhaven	10 January 1955
		Wemyss Castle	10 January 1955
Stations closed	*Date*	West Wemyss	7 November 1949
Methil	10 January 1955		

The closed station of Buckhaven, looking east, March 1958.

Methil was once a fairly large port, its main export being coal, and in 1889 the North British bought both the railway and Methil docks, both of which had been the property of Captain Wemyss of Wemyss Castle. In 1881 the line only went as far as Buckhaven but it was extended to Methil six years later. At Methil it continued northwards to join the Thornton Junction - St Andrews line just outside Leven Station but this section never carried any passenger services. For a number of years the passenger service was operated by a Sentinel railcar as passenger traffic on the line was fairly light. The railcar was named *Bridge of Don* and was put into service by the London and North Eastern Railway Company (who had taken over from the North British following the Railways Act of 1921) from the period January 1931 until January 1944. It could carry 59 passengers and was based at Thornton Junction shed.

In the middle 1920s there were six daily return journeys between Thornton Junction and Methil with the five and a quarter mile trip taking about 20 minutes. These services lasted right up until the line was closed to passengers. Freight traffic along the line lasted until the mid-1960s.

Class 4MT, 2-6-0, no. 76113, passing the closed station of Wemyss Castle with empty wagons, March 1958.

Newburgh (Glenburnie Junction) - St Fort (North Junction)

Passenger service withdrawn	12 February 1951	*Stations closed*	*Date*
Distance	13.25 miles	Lindores	12 February 1951
		Luthrie	12 February 1951
		Kilmany	12 February 1951

Before closure, Lindores.

This line linked the Perth to Ladybank route with the east coast main line at St Fort. Opened in January 1909, the line was single track but had a number of passing loops. There was also a large number of bridges along the route - 31 in total. The railway was worked by the North British but the owners of the line in its early years were the Newburgh and North Fife Railway Company who were not happy with the North British operation of the line. They alleged that the North British failed to advertise the line, the level of service provided was insufficient and that there were not enough proper connections to other locations. This was illustrated by the Lord Provost of Dundee who stated publicly that many residents of Dundee had never heard of the line. For a short while during the First World War passenger services were withdrawn due to staff shortages but the normal timetable provided for three trains in each direction with an additional one on Saturdays. One service split at St Fort with a portion going to St Andrews, but most trains ran to Dundee.

Passenger numbers were never high and the line did not fulfil its role as a through route. By 1951 there were only two trains per day in each direction. However, it was a favourite line for excursion traffic and the line had a visit by the 'Scottish Rambler' railtour in 1962. Freight services were withdrawn in the early 1960s and the line's final use was as a long siding to hold condemned wagons.

Newport-on-Tay - Dundee (Wormit Junction)

Passenger service withdrawn   5 May 1969   *Stations closed*   *Date*
Distance   3 miles   Newport-on-Tay (East)   5 May 1969

Newport-on-Tay (West)	5 May 1969
Wormit	5 May 1969

Looking towards Tayport from Newport-on-Tay (East), January 1959.

Known as the Newport Railway, this line left the east coast main line at Wormit and rejoined it at Leuchars Junction. Fully operational in 1879, the line initially had four through trains from Leuchars plus thirteen services from Tayport to Dundee. The complete line lost its passenger services in stages: Leuchars Junction to Tayport, 9 January 1956; Tayport to Newport-on-Tay East, 22 May 1966; Newport-on-Tay East to Dundee, 5 May 1969. Wormit Station was situated only yards from the Tay Bridge and was the scene of a serious accident in 1955 when a picnic special returning to Dundee from Tayport overturned at Wormit tunnel, killing three and injuring 42 others. After nationalisation there were about seventeen trains to and from Dundee and with the construction of the Tay Road Bridge in the 1960s, closure of the line became imminent. The original closure date was meant to be 6 January 1969 but was deferred until May 1969 due to a problem with the replacement bus service. The line was lifted shortly afterwards.

Class 4MT, 2-6-4T, no. 80124, at Wormit with the 1.25 p.m. from Tayport to Dundee, November 1962.

North Queensferry - Inverkeithing (South Junction)

Passenger service withdrawn   5 March 1890   *Stations closed*   *Date*

Distance   1.75 miles   North Queensferry   5 March 1890

On 4 March 1890 the Forth Railway Bridge opened to passenger traffic. Prior to this passengers who wished to cross the Firth of Forth travelled by train to North Queensferry where they crossed by ferry. On arrival at South Queensferry they boarded a train for Edinburgh which, travelling via Kirkliston, joined the present-day Edinburgh - Glasgow route at Ratho. The line from North Queensferry rose fairly sharply to Inverkeithing where, with the construction of the Forth Bridge, a new junction was built. Freight trains continued to use the North Queensferry branch until October 1954.

Class B1 4-6-0, no. 61146, at Rosyth Dockyard with a 1.00 p.m. Navy Day excursion from Cardenden, July 1957.

Rosyth Dockyard – Inverkeithing (Naval Base Junction)

Passenger service withdrawn   24 November 1989   *Stations closed*   *Date*

Distance   1 mile   Rosyth Dockyard   24 November 1989

This line was built during the First World War by the Admiralty to serve the naval dockyard at Rosyth. Opened in July 1915, and run by the North British, the line handled special trains to and from the dockyard station. After the war, passenger traffic was limited to workmen's trains, most of which originated at Kirkcaldy. In 1981 excursion trains used the line during open days at the dockyard. The last workmen's train may have run a few years earlier than the official closing date of 1989.

St Andrews - Leuchars (Leuchars South Junction)

Passenger service withdrawn
Distance

6 January 1969   *Stations closed*
5 miles   St Andrews
    Guard Bridge

Date
6 January 1969
6 September 1965

Class B1, 4-6-0, no. 61342, at St Andrews with the 4.13 p.m. to Glasgow (Queen Street) and Class J37, 0-6-0, no. 64575, with the 3.47 p.m. from Leuchars Junction, August 1958.

July 1852 saw the arrival of the railway in St Andrews. The line left the east coast Edinburgh - Dundee main line at Leuchars Junction before heading south east to St Andrews. From there the line extended further south, serving coastal villages such as Anstruther and Crail, before reaching Leven and rejoining the east coast main line at Thornton Junction. St Andrews was well served by trains and at one time it was possible to catch direct trains to Perth, Glasgow, Edinburgh and Dundee. Latterly, services were reduced to mainly local trips to and from Leuchars Junction/ although some trains occasionally ran to and from Dundee. Freight services were withdrawn in 1962.

Class B1, 4-6-0, no. 61133, at Guard Bridge with the 2.10 p.m. from Dundee to Edinburgh, August 1958.

St Fort: West Junction - South Junction

Passenger service withdrawn   1914   *Distance*   0.5 miles

St Fort was about five miles south of the Tay Bridge on the east coast Dundee - Edinburgh main line and formed a triangular junction with the line from Perth and Newburgh. The majority of services which used this line continued on to Dundee; however, until 1914 there was one four-coach train from Perth which split into two portions at St Fort west signal box, with one going to Dundee and the other to St Andrews. There was a similar return service in the afternoon but this generated very little traffic and was withdrawn shortly after the outbreak of the First World War.

Stirling (Dunfermline Line Junction) - Dunfermline Lower (Touch South Junction)

Passenger service withdrawn	7 October 1968	*Stations closed*	*Date*
Distance	20.25 miles	Clackmannan Road	1 December 1921
		Forest Mill	22 September 1930
Stations closed	*Date*	Bogside (Fife)	15 September 1958
Causewayhead	4 July 1955	East Grange	15 September 1958
Cambus	7 October 1968	Oakley	7 October 1968
Alloa Junction	November 1865	Dunfermline Upper	7 October 1968
Alloa	7 October 1968		

East Grange Station, looking west, September 1958.

This line opened in 1850 and provided the North British with an inroad into the Caledonian Company's territory at Stirling. The line from Dunfermline had connections from the Fife area as well as direct contact with the Devon Valley line from Alloa to Kinross and on to Perth. A short branch line went from Cambus to Alva. There was also a line from Alloa to Culross and onwards to Dunfermline Lower. During the line's heyday in the mid-1920s there were local services between Stirling and Dunfermline, through trains from Stirling to Edinburgh via Alloa, as well as trains from Glasgow to Perth, also via Alloa.

A Type 2 diesel locomotive, no. D5312, at Oakley with the
4.30 p.m. from Stirling to Edinburgh, September 1968.

Class V3, 2-6-2T, no. 67669, at Dunfermline Upper with the 4.25 p.m. from Edinburgh to Stirling, March 1960.

Tayport - Leuchars (Leuchars North Junction)

Passenger service withdrawn	9 January 1956	*Stations closed*	*Date*
Distance	5.5 miles	Leuchars Old	3 October 1921
		Leuchars Junction	1 June 1878

Class B1, 4-6-0, no. 61403, passing the closed station of Leuchars Old with the 2.17 p.m. from Dundee to Edinburgh via Tayport, December 1955.

This section of line formed the southern section of the Newport Railway which ran from Wormit to Leuchars Junction. This allowed the line to leave and rejoin the east coast Dundee - Edinburgh main line at these two locations. The station at Leuchars Junction was closed in June 1878 when the more direct route to Dundee was opened. Latterly, the service level was very basic with only about three return trips daily throughout the whole section of the line from Wormit to Leuchars Junction.

Leuchars Junction, December 1955. On the right is class 4MT, 2-6-4T, no. 80123, with the 1.00 p.m. from Dundee to St Andrews via Tayport, while on the left is class B1, 4-6-0, no. 61402, with the 1.35 p.m. from St Andrews.

Tayport - Newport-on-Tay East

Passenger service withdrawn	22 May 1966	*Stations closed*	*Date*
Distance	2.5 miles	Tay Port	12 May 1879
		Tayport	22 May 1966

A Metro-Cammell DMU arriving at Tayport as the 4.27 p.m. from Dundee, March 1965.

This short section of line formed part of the Newport Railway which ran from Wormit Station to Leuchars Junction. Although through trains between Dundee and Leuchars Junction did operate along the route, most services terminated at Tayport. With the construction of the Tay Road Bridge in the 1960s the threat to the rail passenger service became more pronounced and the line was scheduled for closure in September 1967. However, when part of the rail route was requisitioned for the new approach roads to the bridge, closure was brought forward by more than two years.

Thornton Junction (Central Junction) - Leven

Passenger service withdrawn   6 October 1969   *Stations closed*   *Date*

Distance   5.75 miles   Cameron Bridge   12 May 1879

                                         Leven   22 May 1966

**A Metro-Cammell triple set forming the 12.30 p.m. from
Edinburgh to Leven, Cameron Bridge, August 1969.**

Forming part of the East Coast of Fife line, this route served the' industrial town of Leven as well as the fishing villages situated to the north of it. The section of line from Leven to St Andrews closed in September 1965, leaving a short section from Thornton Junction to Leven. Most trains ran either to Edinburgh or Glasgow.

Class B1, 4-6-0, no. 61103, at Leven with the 2.35 p.m. from
Crail to Thornton Junction, October 1964.

Closed passenger stations on lines still open to passenger services

Line/Service	Edinburgh - Aberdeen

Station	Closure date
Donibristle Halt	2 November 1959
Sinclairtown*	6 October 1969
Dysart	6 October 1969
Thornton Junction	6 October 1969
Falkland Road	15 September 1958
Kingskettle**	4 September 1967
Dairsie	20 September 1954
St Fort	6 September 1965

* Closed from 1 January 1917 until 2 March 1919 except for workmen's trains.
** Closed from 1 January 1917 until 1 February 1919.

The 1.10 p.m. DMU from Edinburgh to Dundee, passing through Donibristle Halt, March 1964.

Class 6MT, 4-6-2, no. 72000 *Clan Buchanan*, at Sinclairtown with the 10.40 a.m. Edinburgh to Dundee sservice, March 1958.

Class B1, 4-6-0, no. 61147, with the 11.30 a.m. Edinburgh to
Thornton Junction service, Dysart, December 1959.

Class J37, 0-6-0, no. 64570, at Dysart with coal from the Frances Colliery, October 1966.

Class B1, 4-6-0, no. 61101, at Thornton Junction with the 11.10 a.m. from Glasgow (Queen Street) to Crail, August 1965.

A Type 4 diesel locomotive, no. D361, passing the closed station of Falkland Road with a southbound freight, March 1965.

Class B1, 4-6-0, no. 61180, at Kingskettle with the 1.07 p.m.
from Dundee to Edinburgh, December 1959.